Table of Contents

INTRODUCTION

Marriage is a universal human institution which has formed the foundation of the family throughout history. While the traditions surrounding marriage ceremonies, the rights and obligations of marriage, the way of choosing one's marriage partner, and even who one is permitted to marry may differ from culture to culture, the essential necessity of marriage has long been recognized economically, legally, spiritually, and socially as the primary social institution for raising children. It is widely recognized that marriage provides the proper setting for cultivating love between a man and a woman, and for the fulfillment of both.

Challenges to the institution of marriage in the twentieth century, although significant and with some limited validity, nonetheless failed to provide a viable alternative. Marriage is the prerequisite for building a family, and the family is the fundamental unit of human society. The future of human society appears to depend more on efforts to understand how to build healthy marriages than on promoting alternatives.

It's a horrible feeling when you recognize that things aren't working in your marriage. A failing marriage is the worst relationship catastrophe that you can imagine. It leaves a trail of pain, anguish, and disenchantment. You may want to be together but feel that there is too much broken or wrong with your relationship to make that happen.

It's not an easy thing to admit that things aren't going well, but the good news is that you can help to get things back on track. You can work through the biggest challenges if you align and address the issues that are bringing you both down.

This will involve both of you and a willingness to admit when your marriage is broken, what went wrong and made you and your spouse bring you to the verge of a broken marriage and then find ways to repair the broken marriage.

CHAPTER ONE

Marriage is usually understood as a relationship of mutual emotional support, merged economics, and a mutually advantageous division of labor, procreation, and successful rearing of children. As anthropologist James Q. Wilson said, "In virtually every society, the family is defined by marriage; that is; by a publicly announced contract that makes legitimate the sexual union of a man and a woman". For these reasons, marriage is predominantly seen as being between one man and one woman. Most of the world's population lives in societies where marriages are overwhelmingly heterosexual and monogamous.

Religions in general endorse heterosexual and monogamous marriages. In the Christian tradition, a "one man one woman" model for the Christian marriage was advocated by Saint Augustine with his influential letter, "The Good of Marriage." In 534 C.E Roman Emperor Justinian I criminalized all but monogamous man/woman sex within the confines of marriage. The Justinian Code was the basis of European law for 1,000 years. Christianity has continued to insist on monogamy as essential to marriage.

Globally, most existing societies have embraced heterosexual monogamy as the norm for marriage. However, most societies have at least some history of allowing polygamy, and some still do. Polygamy has usually been limited to polygyny—multiple wives—as opposed to polyandry—multiple husbands. The prevalence of polygyny can probably be explained by the need to ensure many offspring.

The state of matrimony

In modern times, the term "marriage" is generally reserved for a union that is formally recognized by the state. The phrase "legally married" can be used to emphasize this point. In most cases, receiving state recognition of a marriage involves obtaining a marriage license and is subject to certain laws.

In many societies, official approval for marriage may be given by either a religious or civil body. Sociologists thus distinguish between a "marriage ceremony" conducted under the auspices of a religion and a state-authorized "civil marriage."

In Europe the churches were traditionally responsible for make marriages official by registering them. Hence, it was a significant step towards a clear separation of church and state, and also an intended and effective weakening of the Christian churches' role in Germany, when Chancellor Otto von Bismarck introduced the Zivilehe (civil marriage) in 1875. This law made the declaration of the marriage before an official clerk of the civil administration (both spouses affirming their will to marry) the procedure to make a marriage legally valid and effective, and it reduced the clerical marriage to a mere private ceremony.

Civil marriages may be permitted in circumstances which are not allowed by many religions, such as same-sex marriages or civil unions. Marriage may also be created by the operation of the law alone as in common-law marriage, which is a judicial recognition that two people living as domestic partners are entitled to the effects of marriage. Conversely, there are examples of people who have a religious ceremony that is not recognized by the civil authorities. Examples include widows who stand to lose a pension if they remarry and so undergo a marriage in the eyes of God, homosexual couples, some sects of Mormonism which recognize polygamy, retired couples who would lose pension benefits if legally married, Muslim men who wish to engage in polygamy that is condoned in some situations under Islam, and immigrants who do not wish to alert the immigration authorities that they are married either to a spouse they are leaving behind or because the complexity of immigration laws may make it difficult for spouses to visit on a tourist visa.

Weddings

The ceremony in which a marriage is enacted and announced to the community is called a wedding. A wedding in which a couple marries in the "eyes of the law" is called a civil marriage. Religions also facilitate weddings, in the "eyes of God." In many European and some Latin American countries, when someone chooses a religious ceremony, they must hold that ceremony separate from the civil ceremony. Certain countries, like Belgium and the Netherlands even legally demand that the civil marriage has to take place before any religious marriage. In some countries, notably the United

States, the United Kingdom, the Ireland, and Spain, both ceremonies can be held together; the officiant at the religious and community ceremony also serves as an agent of the state to enact the civil marriage. This does not mean that the state is "recognizing" religious marriages, just that the "civil" ceremony takes place at the same time as the religious ceremony. Often this involves simply signing a register during the religious ceremony. If that civil element of the full ceremony is left out for any reason, in the eyes of the law, no marriage took place, irrespective of the holding of the religious ceremony.

In many jurisdictions, the civil marriage ceremony may take place during the religious marriage ceremony, although they are theoretically distinct. In most American states, the marriage may be officiated by a priest, minister, or religious authority, and, in such a case, the religious authority acts simultaneously as an agent of the state. In some countries, such as France, Germany and Russia, it is necessary to be married by the state before having a religious ceremony.

Some countries, such as Australia, permit marriages to be held in private and at any location. Others, including England, require that the civil ceremony be conducted in a place specially sanctioned by law (i.e. a church or registry office), and be open to the public. An exception can be made in the case of marriage by special emergency license, which is normally granted only when one of the parties is terminally ill. Rules about where and when persons can marry vary from place to place. Some regulations require that one of the parties reside in the locality of the registry office.

The way in which a marriage ceremony is enacted has changed over time, as has the institution of marriage itself. In Europe during the Middle Ages, marriage was enacted by the couple promising verbally to each other that they would be married to each other; the presence of a priest or other witnesses was not required if circumstances prevented it. This promise was known as the "verbum." As part of the Reformation, the role of recording marriages and setting the rules for marriage passed to the state. By the 1600s, many of the Protestant European countries had heavy state involvement in marriage.

Termination

Many societies provide for the termination of marriage through divorce. Marriages can also be annulled, or cancelled, which is a legal proceeding that establishes that a marriage was invalid from its beginning.

Rights and obligations relating to marriage

Typically, marriage is the institution through which people join their lives together in emotional and economic ways through forming a household. It often confers rights and obligations with respect to raising children, holding property, sexual behavior, kinship ties, tribal membership, relationship to society, inheritance, emotional intimacy, and love.

Traditionally, marriage has been a prerequisite for starting a family, which then serves as the building block of a community and society. Thus, marriage not only serves the interests of the two individuals, but also the interests of their children and the society of which they are a part.

In most of the world's major religions, marriage is traditionally a prerequisite for sexual intercourse. Unmarried people are not supposed to have a sexual relationship, which is then called fornication and is socially discouraged or even criminalized. Sexual relations with a married person other than one's spouse, called adultery, is even less acceptable and has also often been considered a crime. This is especially true in the case of a person who is a representative of the government (such as a president, prime minister, political representative, school teacher, or military officer).

Marriage may also carry the following rights and obligations, although no society has all, and none are universal:

• establishing the legal father of a woman's child

• establishing the legal mother of a man's child

• giving the husband or his family control over the wife's sexual services, labor, and/or property

• giving the wife or her family control over the husband's sexual services, labor, and/or property;

establishes a joint fund of property for the benefit of children

• establishing a relationship between the families of the husband and wife.

Religious views of marriage

Many religions have extensive teachings regarding marriage. In the Christian tradition, marriage is to be a union of mutual love and support. God created the institution of marriage when He gave the first woman to the first man. Marriage can only be the union of one man and one woman. The Bible states in Genesis 2:24, "Therefore a man shall leave his father and his mother and hold fast to his wife, and they shall become one flesh." Though the wife is commanded to submit to her husband, the husband is commanded to love his wife even to the point of giving up his life for her. The Apostle Paul writes in Ephesians 5:22-31:

Wives, submit to your own husbands, as to the Lord. For the husband is the head of the wife even as Christ is the head of the church, his body, and is himself its Savior. Now as the church submits to Christ, so also wives should submit in everything to their husbands. Husbands love your wives, as Christ loved the church and gave himself up for her, that he might sanctify her, having cleansed her by the washing of water with the word, so that he might present the church to himself in splendor, without spot or wrinkle or any such thing, that she might be holy and without blemish. In the same way husbands should love their wives as their own bodies. He who loves his wife loves himself. For no one ever hated his own flesh, but nourishes and cherishes it, just as Christ does the church, because we are members of his body. Therefore a man shall leave his father and mother and hold fast to his wife, and the two shall become one flesh. This mystery is profound, and I am saying that it refers to Christ and the church. However, let each one of you love his wife as himself, and let the wife see that she respects her husband.

Most Christian churches give some form of blessing to a marriage; the wedding ceremony typically includes some sort of pledge by the community to support the couple's relationship. In the Roman

Catholic Church, "Holy Matrimony" is considered to be one of the seven sacraments and has been so since the twelfth century. The sacrament is one that the spouses bestow upon each other in front of a priest and members of the community as witnesses during a "Nuptial Mass." This is also true of other Orthodoxies, where marriage is defined as a relationship between a man and a woman. In the Eastern Orthodox Church, it is one of the "Mysteries," and is seen as an ordination and martyrdom. In marriage, Christians see a picture of the relationship between Jesus and the Church. The Protestant Reformation reformulated marriage as a life-long covenant that should not be entered into lightly.

In Judaism, marriage is viewed as a coming together of two families, therefore prolonging the religion and cultural heritage of the Jewish people. Islam also recommends marriage highly; among other things, it helps in the pursuit of spiritual perfection. The Bahá'í Faith sees marriage as a foundation of the structure of society, and considers it both a physical and spiritual bond that endures into the afterlife. Hinduism sees marriage as a sacred duty that entails both religious and social obligations. By contrast, Buddhism does not encourage or discourage marriage, although it does teach how one might live a happily married life.

Religious views of the end of marriage

It is also worth noting that different religions have different beliefs regarding the breakup of marriage. For example, the Roman Catholic Church does not permit divorce, because in its eyes, a marriage is forged by God. The Church states that what God joins together, humans cannot put asunder. As a result, people who obtain a civil divorce are still considered married in the eyes of the Catholic Church, which does not allow them to remarry in the Church, even if they participate in a civil marriage. In some special cases, however, Catholics can be permitted an annulment, which declared the marriage to be invalid.

Islam does allow divorce; however, there is a verse stated in the Qur'an describing divorce as the least desirable act allowed between people. The general rule is for a man to allow his wife to stay until the end of her menstrual period or for three months, if she so wishes, after the divorce. During this period they would be divorced in that they would simply be living under the same roof but not functioning as man and wife. The Qur'an scholars suggest that the main point is to prevent any decisions by the woman from being affected by hormonal fluctuations, as well as to allow any heated arguments or differences to be resolved in a civil manner before the marriage is completely terminated. However, there is no obligation on the woman to stay; if she so wishes she may leave. The man is also obligated to give his wife a gift or monetary sum equivalent to at least half her mahr (gift or monetary sum which is given to the wife at the commencement of the marriage). Specific conditions as to how a divorce is conducted also apply if a woman is pregnant, or has given birth just prior to the divorce.

Marriages are typically entered into with a vow that explicitly limits the duration of the marriage with the statement "till death do you part." However, the Church of Jesus Christ of Latter-day Saints (the Mormons) have a distinctive view of marriage called "Celestial marriage," wherein they believe that worthy individuals can enter into a marriage relationship that endures beyond death.

The Unification Church of Reverend Sun Myung Moon also asserts that marriage is eternal.

Marriage and economics

The economics of marriage have changed over time. Historically, in many cultures the family of the bride had to provide a dowry to pay a man for marrying their daughter. In other cultures, the family of the groom had to pay a bride price to the bride's family for the right to marry the daughter. In some cultures, dowries and bride prices are still demanded today. In both cases, the financial transaction takes place between the groom (or his family) and the bride's family; the bride has no part in the transaction and often no choice in whether or not to participate in the marriage.

In most subsistence societies, children are a financial asset because they can work in the family farm or business. In modern urban industrial life, children have become viewed as an economic liability and as preventing both parents from working. As a result, adults are choosing to have less children causing families to be much smaller, and sometimes just the husband and wife.

In many modern legal systems, two people who marry have the choice between keeping their property separate or combining it. In the latter case, called community property, when the marriage ends by divorce each owns half. If one partner dies, the surviving partner owns half, and for the other half, inheritance rules apply.

In some legal systems, the partners in a marriage are "jointly liable" for the debts of the marriage. This has a basis in a traditional legal notion called the "Doctrine of Necessities" whereby a husband was responsible to provide necessary things for his wife. The respective maintenance obligations during and eventually after a marriage, such as alimony, are regulated in most jurisdictions.

Whom one may marry—exogamy and endogamy

Societies have always placed restrictions on marriage to close relatives, though the degree of prohibited relationship varies widely. In almost all societies, marriage between brothers and sisters is forbidden and termed incest. Ancient Egyptian,

Hawaiian, and Inca royalty are the rare exception, with this privilege being denied commoners. Thus it may be understood as having served to concentrate wealth and power in one family. In many societies, marriage between some first cousins is preferred, while at the other extreme, the medieval Catholic church prohibited marriage even between distant cousins. The present day Catholic Church still maintains a standard of required distance (in both consanguinity and affinity) for marriage. Genetically, these practices have proven to be healthy for society.

In the Indian Hindu community, especially in the Brahmin caste, marrying a person of the same Gothra is prohibited, since persons belonging to the same Gothra are said to have identical patrilineal descension. In ancient India when Gurukul was in existence, the shishyas (the pupils) were advised against marrying any of Guru's children as shishyas were considered Guru's children and it would be considered marriage among siblings.

Many societies have also adopted other restrictions on whom one can marry, such as prohibitions on marrying persons with the same family name (surname), or persons with the same sacred animal. In Uganda, people are exhorted to marry outside of their own clan. In South Korea it is generally considered taboo for a man to marry a woman if they both have the same family name. A large percentage of the total South Korean population has the surname "Kim" (an estimated 20 percent; rendering 20 percent of the Korean population ineligible for marriage to each other).

Anthropologists refer to these sorts of restrictions, limiting whom one may marry, as exogamy. It has been suggested that the incest taboo may serve to promote social solidarity.

Societies have also at times required marriage from within a certain group. Anthropologists refer to these restrictions as endogamy. An example of such restrictions would be a requirement to marry someone from the same tribe. Racist laws adopted by some societies in the past, such as Nazi-era Germany, apartheid-era South Africa and most of the southern United States and Utah prior to 1967, which prohibited marriage between persons of different races (miscegenation) could also be considered examples of endogamy.

Love and marriage

Most cultures agree that love in marriage is desirable and important. The question of when and how love enters a marriage is less agreed upon. In the Western romantic tradition, a couple meets, falls in love, and marries on the basis of their love. In many Eastern cultures, the marriage between a man and a woman is arranged by parents, elders, religious leaders, or by consensus. It is expected that if both parties live up to their obligations and practice their religion faithfully enough throughout the marriage, love will grow up between them.

Arranged marriages have been practiced in many parts of the world and continue today in some cultures, for example among Hindus and Orthodox Jews. Those who uphold arranged marriage frequently state that it is traditional, that it upholds social morals, and that it is good for the families involved, as there is widespread acceptance of the marriage and an understanding that the marriage is between two families, not only two individuals. They also have some traditional criticisms of romantic marriage, saying that it is short-term, overly based on sexual lust, or immoral. Questioned about such practices, young people participating in arranged marriages often express trust in their parents, who love them and want the best for them and who will choose a good partner for them. They also point to the high divorce rate in Western romantic marriages.

Defenders of romantic marriage would hold that it is preferable to achieve an emotional bond before entering into a lifelong commitment. They speak of the mysterious quality of love that cannot be defined, contained, forced or manufactured. Compatibility is emphasized, which may be where the idea of "trial marriages"—cohabitation undertaken to test out a couple's compatibility, including sexual compatibility—developed.

In the Americas and Europe, the prevailing view toward marriage today and for many centuries has been that it should be based on emotional attachment between the partners and entered into voluntarily. The idea of marriage being based upon emotional attachment, however, allows for divorce and remarriage to be easily undertaken when emotional attachment has changed or faded. It has led to a prevalence of what is called "serial monogamy." Serial monogamy involves entering into successive marriages over time. Serial monogamy is not looked upon with the same favor as lifelong marriage to one partner; however, it is considered morally preferable to sex outside of marriage, which is generally frowned upon, whether it is adulterous or premarital.

Those who believe in romantic marriage will often criticize arranged marriages, even expressing horror at the idea. They consider it oppressive, inhuman, or immoral. Defenders of arranged marriage disagree, often pointing to cultures where the success rate of arranged marriages is seen to be high, and holding that nearly all couples learn to love and care for each other deeply.

Studies of altruism and empathy indicate that people who have strong altruistic feelings toward others in general enjoy "very happy" marriages. Those who cultivate an altruistic, even self-sacrificing, attitude toward their spouses also report "very happy" marriages. The study points out that marital love is both built upon and fosters altruistic love—an idea that is common in many religions. These findings would seem to affirm that if the partners in arranged marriages practice and uphold the tenets of their religion—most of which emphasize altruistic love—they will grow together in love for one another as well.

Marriage preparation

Given that the marriage ceremony is one of the most important rites of passage in most cultures, it is to be expected that a certain amount of preparation is involved. Traditionally, preparation for marriage has involved family, church, and community. Children learn the knowledge and skills to manage a household and support a family from their parents and extended family. When children are raised in communities where their parents and most other adults are married, such practical preparation for marriage occurs naturally.

Spiritual guidance, as well as guidance in relationship development and life skills, may be offered or even required in order to be married in a religious ceremony. The Catholic church, for example, requires couples to attend a marriage preparation workshop, often called a "Pre-Cana," as well as private meetings with the priest to prepare the wedding liturgy and ensure that all the Canon law requirements have been met.

The state also has certain requirements in order to legalize a marriage, which in most countries involves obtaining a marriage license.

Requirements vary, although they typically include many or all of the following: proof of identity, age, residency, a waiting period (which may be as short as one day), parental approval if under a particular age (typically sixteen or eighteen years), a blood test for venereal disease, and payment of a fee. In some cases, the fee and waiting period may be reduced or waived if couples complete an approved marriage preparation course.

While some have argued that prior sexual experience prepares one for the conjugal relationship, in reality this has not been shown to be true. The majority of religions, and an increasing number of psychologists and marriage professionals, recognize that the sexual relationship has life changing consequences for those involved. Apart from the potential for pregnancy and sexually transmitted diseases including AIDS, sexual activity has an emotional and spiritual impact. Once a sexual relationship has been entered into, there is no return to the previously pure state of relating like brother and sister. For this reason, maintaining one's virginity prior to marriage is considered a key component of successful marriage preparation. Programs such as the Christian "True Love Waits" encourage young people to make sexual abstinence part of their marriage preparation by signing this pledge:

Believing that true love waits, I make a commitment to God, myself, my family, my friends, my future mate, and my future children to a lifetime of purity including sexual abstinence from this day until the day I enter a biblical marriage relationship.

Building healthy marriages

With the erosion of marriage in the twentieth century, support for couples preparing for marriage, and continued support during the marriage, is no longer available naturally through their family and community. Instead, couples wishing to build a healthy marriage may participate in programs sponsored by their local church, or by professional marriage counselors.

Key issues that marriage counselors address include sexual relations, relationships with in-laws particularly between the mother-in-law and daughter-in-law, finances, and parenting styles in raising their children. Conflicts also occur when one or both of the spouses have personal problems, such as drug abuse or alcoholism.

Successful marriages take commitment and investment on the part of both spouses. To be successful, marriage partners need to have reached a level of individual maturity, such that they have clarified their own life goals and developed their talents and character sufficiently to be able to pursue them, and to have experienced harmonious relationships with others, such as their parents, extended family members, siblings, and peers. Without this type of foundation, even the most passionate feelings of love are not enough to build a healthy marriage.

Just as sexual purity is considered by many an important part of marriage preparation, fidelity between husband and wife is important in building and maintaining a healthy marriage. Adultery has been condemned by many religions, criminalized by many societies, and has led to the downfall of many great historical figures as well as the breakdown of numerous marriages. Healthy marriages are based on trust and commitment; "cheating" on one's spouse violates this relationship in an unforgettable fashion.

Marriage and family

The purpose of marriage is, ultimately, not just for the sake of the man and woman who participate in the union, it is the road to the next generation, children, and the continuation of one's lineage. The conjugal relationship of husband and wife is the emotional and physical foundation for building a family, in which children, produced through the love of man and woman, are nurtured and protected until they reach maturity, and embark on their own lives, which also involve the continuation of the lineage.

The family, formed through the marriage of man and woman and resulting in children, is a universal institution in human life:

As far back as our knowledge takes us, human beings have lived in families. We know of no period where this was not so. We know of no people who have succeeded for long in dissolving the family or displacing it.... Again and again, in spite of proposals for change and actual experiments, human societies have reaffirmed their dependence on the family as the basic unit of human living—the family of father, mother and children.

Civilized society is built upon the family: "the family is the culture-creating institution par excellence". Children naturally inherit not only their physical characteristics as well as physical and material wealth, they also receive their social heritage from their biological parents. The family, therefore, is the social structure most effective in passing on traditions, beliefs, and values from one generation to the next.

Beyond the benefit received through these different types of inheritance, children raised in a stable family by their married parents, have been found, on average, to be "physically and mentally healthier, better educated, and later in life, enjoy more career success than children in other family settings". On the other hand, children of divorce, single-parent families, and step-families are considerably more likely to have emotional and behavioral problems—they sometimes fail to graduate high school, abuse drugs and alcohol, engage in sexual activity as teenagers, suffer unwanted pregnancies, are involved in violence and crime, avoid marriage and child-bearing, get divorced, and commit suicide at higher rates than those raised by two married parents.

Good marriages and the resulting families have been, and continue to be, essential to the social fabric of human society. Without marriage there is no stability in the family, and without stable families the next generation is at grave risk in all aspects of life.

Challenges to traditional assumptions about marriage

In the latter decades of the twentieth century many traditional assumptions about the nature, purpose, and definition of marriage and family were challenged. These challenges ran parallel to dramatic increases in divorce (from 6 percent to over 40 percent of first marriages), cohabitation without marriage, a growing unmarried population, and children born outside of marriage (from 5 percent to over 33 percent of births), as well as an increase in adultery (8 percent to over 40 percent).

Cohabitation is on the rise worldwide. It has been argued that marriage may be an unnecessary legal fiction—the proverbial "piece of paper"—and that living together is just as viable an option for men and women who wish to have a sexual relationship. Studies show, however, that marriage differs considerably from cohabitation. People who live together before they marry are much more likely to divorce later on than people who did not live together before their marriage. In some countries, like Sweden, the divorce rate for women who cohabited before marriage is 80 percent higher than for women who did not cohabit before marriage. These findings have been repeated in other countries. What is more, cohabitation does not bring the same benefits to children's well-being as marriage does. In England, one study showed that children who lived with cohabiting rather than married parents are twenty times more likely to become victims of child abuse. Children of cohabiting couples also experience more poverty and disruption in their future relationships.

Feminists have argued that marriage was part of patriarchy and designed to oppress and abuse women. Some social scientists agreed, seeing traditional marriages and the families formed under them as dysfunctional almost by definition. Divorce was seen as a step toward liberation.

There is, no doubt, much truth to the criticism that marriage was part of the general oppression of women. In many areas of the world, when a woman was in her early teens her father arranged a marriage for her in return for a bride price, sometimes to a man twice her age who was a stranger to her. Her older husband then became her guardian and she could be cut off almost completely from her family. The woman had little or no say in the marriage negotiations, which might even have occurred without her knowledge.

Some traditions allowed a woman who failed to bear a son to be given back to her father. This reflected the importance of bearing children and extending the family to succeeding generations.

Often both parties have expected to be virgins before their marriage, but in many cultures women were more strictly held to this standard. One old tradition in Europe, which survived into the twentieth century in rural Greece, was for this to be proven by hanging the bloody bed sheet from the wedding night from the side of the house. Similarly, sexual fidelity is very often expected in marriage, but sometimes the expectations and penalties for women have been harsher than those for men.

In some traditions marriage could be a traumatic, unpleasant turn of events for a girl. "The Lot of Women" written in Athens in the mid fifth century B.C.E. laments this situation:

Young women, in my opinion, have the sweetest existence known to mortals in their father's homes, for their innocence always keeps children safe and happy. But when we reach puberty and can understand, we are thrust out and sold away from our ancestral gods and from our parents. Some go to strange men's homes, others to foreigner's, some to joyless houses, some to hostile. And all this once the first night has yoked us to our husband we are forced to praise and say that all is well.

On the other hand, marriage has often served to assure the woman of her husband's continued support and enabled her to focus more attention on the raising of her children. This security has typically been greater when and where divorce has been more difficult to obtain.

Although in some cultures marriage has led to the abuse of women, in fact, modern women and their children are more likely to be abused in a cohabitation situation or by members of a stepfamily they have become part of after a divorce. The data pouring in, even through some former advocates of "no-fault" divorce like Judith Wallerstein, strongly show that children's well-being depends heavily upon the long-term, committed involvement of their biological parents with one another and with them. There is a growing consensus among social scientists that society cannot exist without a substantial mass of intact marriages and families built on the traditional model—that is, mutually monogamous marriage between one man and one woman who then care for and raise their children together.

Some people have chafed under the constraints of monogamy and advocated "open marriages" or "swinging" as an alternative to traditional marriage. They have agreements with their spouses that permit other intimate relationships or sexual partners without considering this the abrogation of the marriage. However, as psychologist Carl Rogers noted and James Q. Wilson also stressed, dealing with such arrangements without jealousy, emotional pain, and severe misunderstandings is highly problematic for most people.

Gay rights advocacy groups have disagreed with the notion that marriage should be exclusively between a man and a woman. Due to their lobbying efforts, same-sex marriages are now legal in some countries such as Belgium, the Netherlands, Spain, and Canada. Same-sex unions have been recorded in the history of a number of cultures, but marriages or socially-accepted unions between same-sex partners were rare or nonexistent in other cultures. Same-sex marriage remains infrequent worldwide.

"Civil unions" are recognized

In Denmark, Norway, Sweden, Finland, Greenland, Iceland, Germany, France, Portugal, New Zealand, the United Kingdom, and certain states in the United States. Also, various localities recognize domestic partnerships, which offer parity of spousal rights, to different degrees, with marriage.

Legal response to challenges to marriage

These developments have created a political backlash, most notably in Great Britain, where the Church of England has officially banned gay marriage, and in the United States, where several states have specifically outlawed same-sex marriage, often by popular referenda.

At the United States federal level, the Defense of Marriage Act (DOMA) of 1996 created a federal definition of marriage as between a man and a woman, as well as allowing states to refuse to recognize a same-sex marriage recognized by another state.

Sociologist David Court wright maintains that violence and crime are directly related to men remaining single. He suggests that marriage channels male aggressiveness into positive social roles—such as supporting and rearing a family— and validates masculinity in a way that negates the need for "honor killings" and other violent behavior. Married men have more reason for self-control. They avoid fights, consume less alcohol and drugs, and stay steadily employed. They are stakeholders in a community they want to be stable for their wives and children. Indeed, Court wright relates the most violent eras and locations in United States history to a prevalence of single males. He cites the examples of the Gold Rush in the wild West, where a dearth of females in the early years meant skyrocketing homicide rates, and the modern urban ghetto where marriage is not a norm and where many single young men behave in dangerous, destructive, and self-destructive ways.

In her seminal book, The Case for Marriage, Linda J. Waite, professor of sociology at the University of Chicago, maintains that married people are emotionally, psychologically, and physically healthier than their divorced, bereaved, or single counterparts. When illness of any sort does occur, married people recover more quickly and thoroughly than those without a supportive partner. Married couples in cross-cultural studies are also better off financially than their divorced, bereaved, or single counterparts. Social scientists in the United States have increasingly found that married-to-one-another parents provide for their biological children's well-being in ways that no other social structure has yet to attain.

Marriage has been found to contribute to social stability in other countries as well. Studies in England and Germany have shown that rising divorce rates led young men into increased criminality, drug abuse and general disorder. Crime rates in general have been shown to be directly related to the state of marriage in a community: the more divorced people, single parents and single people in communities, the higher the crime rates.

Anthropologist Margaret Mead once quipped, "The problem in any society is what to do with the men." Socially speaking, the best answer seems to be: marry them.

CHAPTER TWO

How Women Hurt Their Husbands

While both husband and wife should take responsibility for their part in a marriage, below are twelve mistakes common to women, which can completely destroy a marriage. When women exercise the following behaviors, it can create a hostile environment, where no one feels safe or comfortable. There are also plenty of ways that men can destroy a marriage as well.

It is important to remember that the main goal of marriage should be peace and happiness. If life is stressful, then work on changing your perception and start making positive changes in your life.

You can see peace instead of stress. You are only one thought away from a peaceful life. If you feel unhappy, seek the things that will fulfill you in life. Just be happy. The only person you can change is yourself.

1. Using Words to Hurt, Maim, and Destroy Your Marriage

Women are adept at brandishing the sharpest words in order to shame, demean, and belittle their man. Words are like toothpaste, once they are out, there is no getting them back in. Regardless of how sorry you are afterward, the damage has been done. All the sorries in the world will never take back the sting of your angry words, once you have unleashed them on your hapless husband. Over the years, this type of constant verbal abuse can wear on your husband and make him very unresponsive to you and care less about you.

Rather than use your words as a weapon, use them as a healing balm to comfort, encourage and uplift your husband. And as grandma always used to say, "If you can't say something nice, then don't say anything at all."

2. Having Unrealistic Expectations

Seeking fulfillment from one person, and projecting your unhappiness onto him when he doesn't measure up will quickly destroy your marriage. If you feel unhappy, first examine reality. You will be happier if you shape your expectations to fit the reality of your situation. Expecting your spouse or children to make you happy is unrealistic. Make yourself happy.

Imagine if you could only have one friend for your entire life. Would that work for you? Most women have several friends, who fill several roles. We have a friend with whom we like to go shopping. One friend likes to work out with us. One friend leads a bible study. One friend loves to have coffee on Wednesday mornings.

Each person in your life fulfills a different and important role. None is more important; they are just different. If you expect your husband to complete you and bring you eternal happiness, not only are you setting him up for failure, but you are also setting yourself up for disappointment.

Rather than look to one person to fulfill your every need, try expanding your circle of influence, to include a variety of people, who fill your life with different blessings. And most of all, look to yourself. Find ways to feel complete and happy with who you are as a person. First, seek to find your own happiness, within yourself. Then, rather than look to someone else to complete you, find ways to complement each other's lives.

3. Using Sarcastic and Critical Statements, Gestures, and Facial Expressions

This is a quick and easy way to show your husband that you don't respect him or his opinion. Men can become overwhelmed by the barrage of criticism coming at them. The result is they shut down, withdraw, and seek kindness and approval elsewhere.

Have you ever experienced someone discounting what you have to say, without actually listening to you? When you are critical or sarcastic with your husband, he feels attacked and unvalued. Listen to him, without adding your two cents worth. If you'd like to ask questions, wait until he stops talking. Don't interrupt with a story about how the dog threw-up on the carpet. Let him have a few minutes to be the center of your attention. And if you absolutely must get dinner made, invite him to join you in the kitchen. Tell him that you would like to hear about the rest of his day, and mean it.

Another way to show disrespect is to roll your eyes or make sarcastic facial expressions. These are just as irritating for your husband, as they are for you when your teenaged daughter does it. There is no need to be rude, even if you've been married forever. It is more important to give him your attention, to look at him and to listen than it is to roll your eyes or shake your head in exasperation. You are trying to build a bond, not destroy the man you love.

4. Criticizing, Belittling, and Making Fun of Him to Your Friends and Family

When you criticize and belittle your husband, you not only diminish your husband in your eyes, but you also poison those closest to you. You force them to take sides, and of course, they choose your side, because they want to be loyal to you. Your friends and family don't live at your house. They don't see what goes on day after day. They don't see the good things your husband does. The only view they have of your husband is the one that you present to them. If you are constantly badmouthing and belittling him, then they will view him as a bad partner for you.

After you speak badly about him, they will never look at your husband the same way again. Even when you get over your tirade, and everything is great at home, they will still be mad at him. Your friends and family members want to protect you from danger and harm. If you are constantly referring to your husband in a negative light, then they will want to protect you and your children from this monster you married, even if he isn't really a monster.

When you speak poorly of your spouse, your close friendships and relationships will remain irreparably altered against your husband, in time, this can destroy your marriage. He will never understand why your friends don't like him, and why your mother is mean to him.

Rather than trying to make excuses, don't start down that path. When you speak of your husband, use uplifting, encouraging words. If he is acting like a jerk, you don't need to gush about it to everyone you know. Your constant complaints against him will create a wall between your husband and your friends, which he can never overcome.

5. Withholding Affection and Sex

This can cause a huge rift in your marriage, whether you realize it or not. Men are wired differently than women. Your husband needs physical release through sexual intimacy. It is not just something he is demanding of you; it is something he needs, physiologically speaking.

When you refuse to meet his need for physical release, you are making a much deeper statement; you do not care about or respect his needs. This is not about whether you like or dislike sex. It is much more important than that. Your spouse needs to connect with you on a physical level, whether you are in the mood or not.

As much as you need emotional release and closeness, he is wired to need physical release and closeness. Neither is wrong. You are just different. While you want your emotional needs met, it is important not to lose sight of his needs. Think of it this way; what if he stopped talking to you for three days? How about a week? What if he didn't talk to you for an entire month? Unconscionable, right? Likewise, it is unfair for you to cut him off from what he needs. You are in a relationship with a man you love, and you expect your needs to be met. In the same way, you need to meet his needs, regardless of whether you share the same needs and desires.

Men and women are different on many levels. Men are fixers. By nature, if you present a problem, he will come up with concrete steps to solve the problem. When you are dismissive, it sends the message that you do not value him. When you come to your husband with a problem or a concern, be ready for him to create an action plan to resolve your conflict. It may not be exactly what you would do, but he is offering a solution. The least you can do is listen to his suggestion, and thank him for his input. Before you reject his idea out of hand, take some time to consider what his opinion is. Think about what he said. You don't have to do everything he suggests, but listen and think about it.

If you just want to bitch and complain, call a girlfriend. Girlfriends are great listeners. They will not try to fix you. Women like to talk things out, without being fixed. Sometimes you just need an ear to listen, not a solution. When that is the case, perhaps your husband isn't the person to approach.

If you must whine at your husband, tell him upfront that you don't require a solution, just an ear to hear. He will still offer suggestions, but if you tell him, before you begin your rant, that you don't need an answer, just to vent, then he won't be offended when you don't take his advice. And sometimes, you could surprise him and actually follow his advice. It might just work.

7. Undermining His Authority, but Demanding He Take Full Responsibility

In any organization, there must be a leader, someone in charge. The head over the whole organization, who says, "The buck stops here." Typically, the person who carries the responsibility ought to be the one who has the final say. Families and relationships are much like any other organization. There must be someone in charge, someone who will take full responsibility when things go wrong, and someone that everyone can turn to.

You, of course, are welcome to take that role, if you are willing to be fully responsible when the chips are down. It is easy to be critical of the person in charge, and it is easy to think that you could do a better job. The hard part comes when it is time to take responsibility. Rather than making decisions without regard for your husband's input, and then blaming him when things don't work out, try instead to work together. You can decide together how things should be done, and you can offer him the final say when decisions need to be made.

Don't become so focused on your own feelings and fears (i.e. I'm afraid he'll make a bad decision. I feel like I make better decisions) to override his feelings and fears (i.e. I am responsible to take care of the family. I'm afraid no one in the family respects me.) Be gracious in light of his decision making. You can respectfully disagree with a decision without attacking his ability to lead.

8. Never Being Happy

One of the quickest ways to destroy your marriage is to spend all your time acting miserable and unhappy. The goal of marriage should be peace and happiness. It is to this end that you have an obligation to be happy. If the goal is to be happily married, it is up to you to exercise self-control. Only you can make yourself happy. If you believe that your happiness comes from other people or having things or external circumstances, then you will never be happy.

You are in charge of your happiness. It is a decision. You can choose to be a miserable, unhappy grouch, or you can suck it up, pull your boots on, and show up in your marriage as the person you'd like to be.

There is no need to express every angry, bitter or resentful thought. Everybody gets pissed off, frustrated, and irritated. There isn't anyone to blame. You are choosing to respond to your circumstances with that attitude. You can choose a different path. By owning your own problems, you can take responsibility for your own happiness. Each day, work on bringing your best self into the relationship. Regardless of what happens, you are only one thought away from peace.

Remind yourself every day; I can see peace instead of this. And then, work to see the peace that is available to you.

If asked, most men believe their wives to be more moral and spiritual than themselves. Often, the wife agrees. She does not see herself as sinful or wrong. She feels her greatest "sins" lie in being deeply disappointed by her husband's failures and her children's shortcomings. Beyond this, wives typically admit to bad behavior and attitudes but attribute it to hormones, chemical imbalances, and a dysfunctional childhood.

Woe to the husband who dares suggest his lovely bride could use improvement in some aspect of her life. Labeled a heartless, uncaring, unrighteous lout, he is silenced by an angered, wounded wife, cloaked in self-righteous indignation. She then feels perfectly justified in attacking every flaw, magnifying every misstep, and pointing out every failure, until he feels ashamed for living. You are not your husbands Holy Spirit. Stop trying to correct every little flaw you perceive in his character and set about removing the blinding plank from your own eye.

Of course, everyone makes mistakes. You can build him up or tear him down. The choice belongs entirely to you.

You repeat the pattern again, and again. You meet a man, you like him, you start dating. Then you begin to notice the tiny flaws, the chinks in his armor. He yells, just like your Dad did. He drinks and becomes abusive. He is mean to your kids. "It's o.k.," you tell yourself, "I'll fix him after we get married."

Stop right there. There is no fixing it!

The man you date will be the same man after you are married. Inherently kind? He'll still be kind. Addicted to pornography? He'll still be addicted. You cannot change the basic nature of other people. You cannot love them into changing. You cannot nag, or pout, or complain them into changing. If the relationship feels unhealthy during dating, getting married will not fix it. He will not magically become more responsible, more reliable, or more loving after you marry him. So if you want a good husband, find a good man, date him, and marry him.

While this list may seem daunting, it is important to remember that the main goal of marriage should be peace and happiness. If life is stressful, work on changing your perception. You can see peace instead of stress. You are only one thought away from a peaceful life. If you feel unhappy, seek those things that will fulfill you in life. Just be happy. The simplest route to something is to just be. The only person you can change is yourself.

11. Focusing on Work Over the Marriage

It can be easy to fall into the trap of spending too much time at work and not enough time at home. This neglect can have a negative impact on a marriage. While it is hard to find that proper balance between work and home life, focusing on your marriage is still important. Your husband wants to spend time with you, and depriving him of that time so you can focus on your work will cause some friction and resentment.

If you don't give the time of day to your husband and the two of you never see each other due to work commitments, your marriage will be on the rocks very quickly. Many women fall into this trap because they want to focus on bettering their careers. It can be hard to make the time to be with your husband when you are working a full-time job, but if you are serious about maintaining your marriage, you'll have to find a way to make it work.

12. Cheating

I think this goes without saying, but if you cheat on your husband, you will ruin your marriage. There are some lines that cannot be crossed, and that is one of them: infidelity is a big deal-breaker, and your husband will not be able to forgive you for such an act.

HOW TO PROPERLY TRAIN A WIFE

The techniques I use come after nearly twelve years of trial and error in my own marriage. The list does not include everything important, but enough to give you a good start on the training. I hope the ladies who read Inspired-Wife will pass this information on to the men in their lives, so you housewives can also be properly trained.

1. Buy your wife flowers at the grocery store: Really, this training method is cheap, fast and convenient. How many times a week are we men sent out to pick up a gallon of milk, some eggs, or that jar of pickles? How often do we walk right by those grocery store flowers without a glance? Housewives love flowers, whether or not they are from an expensive florist or from a cheaper venue like the grocery store. A nice habit to get into is to buy a bunch of flowers just to brighten the house. Generally, I do this a couple of times a month. These flowers do not even need to be roses. Those five to ten dollar arrangements of flowers will do fine. They will brighten a wife's day and week.

2. If you have kids, hire a babysitter and go on a date: Every wife dreams of escaping the clutches of the household walls. She sweats as she does the dishes, while she cleans the kids' and your pee around the toilet seat, and then folds mountains of hot laundry before it wrinkles. All this time she hangs onto the hope of a single night out alone with her husband. So, spend that fifty to a hundred dollars, and get a good babysitter for a long date somewhere. Take her out to eat, and then maybe walk with her on the boardwalk or a nearby park just to talk with her and catch up.

Movies stimulate no real conversation, so avoid them.

3. Again, if you have kids, give her every Sunday morning to sleep in late: Okay, I will admit this was not a technique I was real happy to learn. My brother actually taught me this one. Yet, it works very well to train a wife. Believe it or not, she is probably exhausted from the endless care she provides to the children. A wife does need to sleep just as much as you do or more. So, why not split the difference on the weekend. You can sleep in on Saturday and she on Sunday, or vice versa. As an extra-credit wife training technique, while she sleeps, try to clean at least the kitchen until it sparkles, and then if you have time, move onto the bathrooms or other areas. The kids will also appreciate the dad time, and can help to "make Mommy happy" for a few extra cookies that normally are against the rules.

4. Arrange for an all-inclusive spa event: Perhaps you guys out there could be unfamiliar with this method, and might find it a bit intimidating to arrange. It is not that difficult. If your wife is

anything like mine, she enjoys getting her nails, feet, and hair done. Additionally, she likes any sort of massage. The best thing to do is simply ask women at your work where the best place is in terms of a spa for a women to get all these things done at a single time. Their excitement to help is phenomenal. Plan for your wife to be there three to four hours while she has this experience. This is a good time to take the kids out on a dad-only outing. I will admit, this will cost you some money, so it is not something of which to make a habit unless you have more money than I do. It will, however, contribute greatly to a well-trained wife in the end. A surprise like this, where you send her on her merry way to someplace she has no clue about where she goes, brings back a very happy wife as seen in the photos here.

5. Personally lingerie shop for her: Despite the lack of time a wife has to attend to her own beauty, every wife loves to feel beautiful. Pretty clothes are a nice way to do this. Although Wal-Mart is convenient, cheap, and anonymous through the self-checkout line, to properly train a wife, you need to potentially humiliate yourself a wee bit. For some guys, like myself, humiliation

could be normal and no big deal, but for others I do understand the challenge to maintain the manly image. The deal is, if you want to make her feel special, you should put some personal effort and emotion into it. For many of us, Victoria's Secret is readily available at the local mall. If they are not available, there are other online options like Frederick's. The really cool thing is the cute young girls who work at these lingerie stores are more than willing to help you out. Just be up front with them from the beginning, breathe, relax, and tell them you are clueless about lingerie, but would like to purchase your wife something special. They will trip over their own knickers to put together an outfit to make your wife happy, and meet your expectations simultaneously. Again, put a little time, thought and money into it, and it will go a long way to properly train a wife. Oh, if you need some shoes to match . . . .

6. Listen to her closely when she needs to talk: Key to success in your regimen to properly train your wife is to take the time to listen to her. By this, I do not just mean to listen with your ears. Listen carefully to what she says, to what she really means, and to what she needs. I will admit,

sometimes it seems like housewives just whine, but really this is all a plea to be heard, to be truly listened to, and to be taken seriously. Validate what they tell you in some manner. Take those few moments to shut off everything else in the world, to include kids and work, and hear her out. It will make the task of training your wife shorter and easier.

7. Love her: You can accomplish the previous six things, and fail on this one item to lose the entire pedagogic effort. You absolutely cannot properly train a wife without love. It is the essential component, like water is to life. Truly love your wife and show her your love in her own love language. Her efforts to "keep" your house will be to your expectations if you do so. Love for your wife is what matters most! Without it, you remain a student in ill-favor indefinitely.

So, to the guys who read this article, I know you thank me now sincerely from the bottoms of your hearts for this enlightened information, and already the wheels of your minds turn on how you can train your own housewives properly. As for the couch-potato doubters out there who think this is a rant in no way related to how to properly train a wife, I beg the difference as evidenced by the photograph below of my own properly trained wife.

CONCLUSION

A broken marriage is fixable. But there's a slight problem.

First, you have to change your perspective. You have to admit you do not truly know how to be married; and that is not easy to do. But when marriage is working according to design, it will not be chaotic or insecure. What is needed is a new look at your marriage. You need to start seeing what works, and doesn't. Going after this problem, and that one …won't work.

When you know how to build and sustain your marriage it will be fixed and ALL the troubles will evaporate. The hard part is that when you run into trouble your first reaction is to get out of the trouble you are in. It is an emergency. So people try to get out of the immediate danger. Then, they usually relapse, repeat the cycle a few times and end up divorced.

This is where couples counseling fails so many.

Most marriage family therapists don't get at the root causes within the marriage. They ask, "what is going on". But what is going on now doesn't really tell anyone anything.

My way is to deal with the emergencies by using special techniques to stop everything, and while there are no more conflict behaviors distracting you, you learn how to build your marriage the right way. Almost anyone (those who can go on to have a great marriage and those who don't end up divorced) can do this.

Truly, the couples who are successful do not know any special secrets.

They just know marriage is something that has to be approached intelligently and systematically. That is where we come in. The study of marriage is not difficult, but it does take some effort.

Made in the USA
Middletown, DE
05 October 2023

40322919R00036